Prepare to Win

Ten Vital Steps to Expand Your Potential

By Dr. Dave Severson

Proficiency Publishers

prepare-to-win.com

Prepare to Win

Prepare to Win

Ten Vital Steps to Expand Your Potential

By Dr. Dave Severson

The Center for Academic Proficiency

Proficiency Publishers

prepare-to-win.com

copyright 2012 Please do not copy any portion of this work without the written permission of author.

Prepare to Win

Table of Contents

Forward: 7

Chapter 1: Three Ultimate Standards 11

Elite: 13

Profound: 20

Brilliant: 23

Chapter 2: Purpose at Your Heart 33

Chapter 3: Setting Smarter Goals 47

Chapter 4: Articulating Focused Roles 55

Chapter 5: Lightning Decision Making 63

Chapter 6: Service is the Product 71

Chapter 7: Powerful Paradigmatic Proaction 77

Chapter 8: Engineering Lasting Change 91

Chapter 9: Conflict, Power and Politics 101

Chapter 10: Realignments, Alliances and Growth ... 111

Epilog: Ensuring a Lasting Legacy 123

This book is for people who want to make more out of their lives. It is for people who see a need to achieve and thrive. It is for people who strive to make a positive impact in this challenging world.

If you want to be proactive in a reactive world, you need to get there first, be the turn-to expert, and do it with creative and superlative style! You can. Then you will be among the elite, the profound and the brilliant.

Dave Severson, Ed.D.

Forward:

This book is for anyone who wants to make a difference in this world. As you go through this book methodically, you will address each facet of personal/professional development. You may skip chapters to subjects that are most pertinent to your immediate situation. After that, fill in the skipped parts for a full exposure to the composite of experience and advice available here.

This book is designed to help anyone perceive and adapt and lead in response to key indicators in their profession's context. This book is meant to show you how to take those adaptations and leadership insights into brilliant, decontextualized, insightful twists for application in broad ranges, in turn generating their own dynamics.

During the past ten years I have been on the adjunct faculty of a university, teaching students what they need to know for a Masters Degree in administration. During that time, several mentoring needs became glaringly apparent. Those issues are equally significant in any profession, but they do not fit into a university syllabus, so they are presented here. Apply what you read to your own situation, from your own perspective.

I have mentored those students as thoroughly as I could and the students have paid many thousands of dollars to the university to study the formal subjects and the applications of the truths with me.

Those students seemed, for the most part, to have no other source of mentoring that had a promise of personal/professional growth.

Many of the courses were pedantic, so my challenge was always to say, "So what?", and find applications for them to take on a practical project and use it to improve their practices according to the theme of the particular course they were taking.

Those years of mentoring form the basis of this book. It is my attempt to recall what they found useful for their professional practice. I have been an avid reader, and a teacher at all three school levels, elementary, junior high and high school, as vice principal and principal, a special education director, and a public school superintendent with a doctorate in educational leadership.

As a graduate school instructor I have taught classes ranging from research methods and statistics to principles of a democratic society. I have developed an approach to direct explicit instruction in teaching critical thinking curricula for reading comprehension and for preparing written compositions. It is called <u>Figure It Out Faster with the Twelve Bridges to Meaning</u>.

For over 30 years I have been a licensed real estate broker, as well as having a license in insurance. Soon after graduating from university, I resided in three foreign countries including a stint as an administrator for an international Christian organization. So I have some training and some experiences and some insights from many sources, which may be useful to others, in any industry.

Many hard working people today feel that their job security is precarious. They see lay-offs happen around them and wonder if they have invested in their own production value to the extent that they are of more value to their employers than the average anonymous subject of redundancy.

Prepare to Win

As the reader studies the issues in these chapters, many questions are posed. Some space is provided in the text to write immediate thoughts, but it would be useful to keep a notebook near-by to write comments and answers to the questions, in order to collect your own reflective thinking about your calling. Life coaches may want to take one chapter at a time for several weeks or months and work on implementation.

Being among the elite advanced guard, building on a foundation of profound understanding of the organic structure of the industry or the discrete science, and then providing brilliant innovations will advance social progress, and may provide financial and public rewards, as well. That is what this book seeks to help the reader to accomplish.

The higher standards are these:

Elite, Profound, and Brilliant

Lesser standards are unworthy of your time on earth. Your life has the potential of being described as Elite and Profound and Brilliant! The time you live during these few years between school and death is your chance at a magnificent life and here is some guidance on how to grow it and show it. These essential elements are designed for you to expand your potential, to actually implement; so act, and make them real in your life.

The ideas of planning your life and building your capacity are not audacious. Every person leaves a legacy of some kind. Do you want your life to be a string of dependent variables, where you are reacting to your circumstances, or will you build your legacy with independent variables that you deliberately enact?

Prepare to Win

Dynamic determination is the powerhouse for growth. Dynamic means it moves and causes movement, like dynamite. Determination means that there is no hesitation, no reverse nor neutral gear. Dynamic determination has emboldened soldiers, missionaries, and martyrs. It exudes the confidence that says, "Don't get in my way!" It initiates insistent action.

Determine to get started, to think longer, to work smarter, to work harder, to work longer, to use leverage, to be tenacious, to learn constantly, to open your eyes to opportunity and variation, to check reality, and make service to others your primary and fundamental purpose. It is certainly true that becoming significant, dynamic, resilient, and historical is no small job! But if you are going to consume oxygen, why not use it for propulsion?

The use of the Bible to understand issues and methods is additional mentoring, sometimes in this context it is called discipling. Those discipling sections of each chapter will be noted by italic type. Whether or not you are a person of faith, the additional information will probably provide you with additional insight and trigger ideas for application. Reading those parts is highly recommended, but it is your choice. The secular essence of each chapter is presented before the italicized portion.

Prepare to Win

Chapter 1: Three Ultimate Standards

Goals are things you want to accomplish; standards are the level of quality you want for each accomplishment. Lots of people may be pursuing your same goal at an adequate level of performance. If an activity or interest is important to you, you are probably at least average already. If you want to be proactive in a reactive world, you need to exceed, stand out from the others, get there first, and do it with superlative style.

Put more superlatives in your life. Consider the definitions of the three standards of this book. This is the level of standard you should be striving for. Anybody can be mediocre. And anybody can get beyond mediocre. And when you do move beyond, you are not average anymore. But it only takes a nudge to be better than average. Standing one nudge better than average is not taking opportunity very far. It takes a push to move significantly toward excellence. Reach for the higher standard. Keep pushing and moving up, pushing and moving up, and don't stop. That is how your potential expands.

The three essential, superlative characteristics in this book deserve study. Each has deep meaning and each needs to be pursued if you want to approach your potential. Each chapter of this book will return to those lofty standards to challenge you in that particular respect, encouraging you to live a life that in the most positive interpretation could be considered **elite** and **profound** and **brilliant**.

Elite:

People who are among the elite are considered to be in the top few members of a society, with a higher status, expected to take leadership, to represent the interests of the group. As you develop more significant and efficient ways to serve others, you will have to make your own way to the elite level. Actually, society's leaders are not elite individuals. Their primary advantage over you is that they enjoy a position of elite status, beyond the masses, because they arrived there first or uniquely.

So your goal is just to get there, to the position where you are out in front. You will have to move out beyond the masses and the humdrum competition to give your particular method of service room to mature and expand. Are you brave enough to step out by yourself? Most people won't make the effort to move out ahead, so you will find yourself in a very small group of bolder movers and shakers if you do step ahead. Since you know your subject matter, what may seem risky to others who are cautious, should seem like an informed opportunity to you.

Even so, it may take some courage for you to step out in front. But remember that courage is always more productive than caution. Many organizations have been built on the concept that availability is more important than ability. Capability held inactive will never take the day compared with bold action, given the availability to act. Taking action in new areas of activity leads a person to develop capacity as experience grows. You can only build capacity when you engage with your challenges.

When people attend a lecture or take a class, they do not build capacity. They may gain knowledge. When people boldly act on information they have in a difficult or challenging situation it develops their character, as well as their skills. As they gain confidence and see how interactions occur in that tenuous context, they gain greater capacity.

When you are running ahead of the pack, it is like being a trail runner. You do not have cues from others to determine how fast you have to run to hit your intermediate goals. You do not have others to suggest where to avoid holes or to identify places you can take advantage of cutting corners. As a front-runner, when you inadvertently stumble in pot holes, you will have to recover and run that much harder to stay ahead, but that's all a part of being ahead.

Proficient runners will tell you that doing well in a race is more of a head game than a physical challenge. That is why you must take every thought captive and banish doubt and timidity and determine to be a finisher. Even at the cost of a limp, or scars, or the threat of seeing some others finish before you do, make sure that you finish something special, even if it is just for your own sake. Finish, even if you have to say, "I wasn't fast, but I wasn't last." You are still ahead of the timid thousands who never even raced.

Prepare to Win

Actually, speaking directly, not metaphorically, preparing for and participating in half-marathons or marathons will probably do things for your character that will benefit other areas of your life. Do it wisely and safely, with coaching and gradual progress, under medical supervision.

In previous centuries, being in the elite has been largely a matter of inherited social class. Notable exceptions might be those few aggressive political and military personalities who inserted themselves in the events of change. Some historians even believe that history students should learn their field of study based on the personalities of significant figures, since those personalities made a profound effect on the existing social status.

In this century, many of those considered elite have distinguished themselves with the ability to bring together technology and business. Consider the giants in technology and in finance. As the first with innovative technology in information services they have moved out ahead of the average person or the established practice. They live in a world where obsolescence is always biting at their heels. New software applications or the invention of financial devices like derivatives have left the common consumer as ineffectual as medieval peasants trying to defend the castle against new and powerful technologies.

You would benefit by the elitist sense of primacy and urgency. Whatever your avocation, you need to be in the front and you need to be there today. Take charge of your life and move toward the elite.

Dare to be bolder, more audacious, more adventurous, even if your friends start to wonder who you are.

Watch out, because moving out toward the elite means you are sticking your neck out. It is not safe. But there is a key to safety for you. The easiest way to avoid an ego hit is to have a small ego. It takes humility to maintain ego safety, especially when you may not have a support system. Your ego is the only thing that can prevent you from entering what may be an embarrassing situation.

Your pride can stop you from risking failure. If you have ever tried to learn a second language, you know the expectation of embarrassment as you made initial attempts to make sense. The students who are bold and take risks are the ones who learn language most quickly.

If you value risk-taking as a trait, it can mitigate against those other threats to your pride. "At least I tried" is a more noble statement than, "I'll never know because I just couldn't take the chance." Some of the most successful people have treated their failures as foundation rubble upon which to build their future.

There are ways to get some shelter for your ego. Try to find someone, in the family or at church, who can keep saying positive things to you. Be forewarned, though. Your friends or family may not see your potential. They may even laugh at your hopes. Their response may be more about their own insecurity; and their misery loves your company. You can't let that matter. A reality check is one thing; a personal attack is another. Here's the difference.

A reality check is a look at your goals in light of all available data in your context. A reality check is about the logic of your

Prepare to Win

plan sequence. A reality check is about the financial resources that can prudently be accessed. A reality check is a look at the balance with the other obligations that have been posted in your life. A reality check requires you to identify and validate the presence of your personal qualifications and the verification of external signals of opportunity in the context that you need in order to move ahead. You should seek input from people who are knowledgeable about you and your goal. A proverb says, "Wisdom is found among a multitude of counselors." If medical school is out of reach for financial or time reasons, you could still care for people as an LVN, RN or Physician's Assistant.

Whose reality are we checking? You may find a lack of confidence about your plan projected by personal friends and family, but that is not your reality check; it's theirs. They may not be able to look beyond the paradigm of mediocrity and routine behavior. People who are blind to your potential cannot help guide you to wisdom's path.

People in your target industry or current work colleagues will have less bias. They provide the resonating sounding board of industry. They have a sense of "next things." With their counsel, the risky concept that you are considering may then be well-informed and thoroughly defended, not impulsive or irresponsible.

Many people have benefited by using a 360 degree assessment tool. Using one of those questionnaires, colleagues, bosses and employees provide input as to how they see your activities and potentials. While this may be hard on your ego, it may be excellent for directing your next stage of development. Truth is valuable.

Prepare to Win

Many people have made mid-life changes out of desperation or allure. Some have decided to get a doctorate at a university. Some have changed occupations, choosing to use those 40 or more hours each week to do something that is more meaningful to them. Some have cut their work time in half in order to participate in a ministry or a charity with the other half of their time. Nonproductively, some have strayed romantically.

It takes boldness to step out, to move toward the elite. Take that step and let the following chapters help you move toward deep knowledge and superlative expression of what you want your life to say.

Prepare to Win

Your thoughts:

(Space, sometimes a whole page, at the end of every chapter or major section is provided for you to write your own thoughts on what you have just read. Critical thinking is not only logically organized, it is reflective, metacognitive, sensing, open-ended and articulate, and unfortunately, too easily forgotten. So write down your thoughts. They will resonate and become more meaningful for you and it is easier to review them.)

Profound:

People credited with a profound understanding are both deeply knowledgeable about their topic, and they are perceptive to subtle indicators of variation as well as sensing patterns of developing trends. As they analyze their findings and their feelings, they have an almost intuitive understanding of the pace of change, and see not only the early signs and sequences of change, but the implications that project from that source.

Profundity does not come to beginners. There are no profound people, but there are people who seem to be better at profound knowledge in areas of their expertise. You may have heard that the best way to detect counterfeit dollars is to have absolute familiarity with the genuine article. With strong background knowledge, any deviation can be perceived. That is how keenly perceptive you should be in your field of endeavor.

You may be able to discern those subtle, easily overlooked variations through advanced instruments like electron microscopes or through good old lunch-time gossip, depending on whether you are a scientist or a politician. Disaggregation of data with charts and graphic representations may add profound perspectives on realities. Either way, as small variations become confirmed, inferences are made. As those inferences mount up, there may be patterns that are tentative, and later can be confirmed. The ability to clearly see the dimensions of reality while others are still trying to focus on the face of it, takes the profound thinker into the action arena of the elite individuals long before others understand what is happening and where to position themselves.

Profound insights are always contextually embedded and then extended. That's the difference between an observation and an insight. One person may observe a phenomenon and find it curious. Another may find that the detail reveals a previous unrealized issue associated with the context.

Even when successful products have come from accidents, like sticky notes, the accident with the adhesive had no practical significance until it was projected to an appropriate context and application was found. Jumping to conclusions leads one to invest in hunches, and there is little market value to hunches.

The fact that perceptions are context-related helps assure that any intervention is supported by the structure of the context. Without that contextual awareness, any interaction would seem to be a cancellation or an interruption, not a participation in the rhythm of the development. Like a martial arts aficionado, the individual who is a profound thinker attempts to use existing rhythms and available momentum to help propel innovation to some new and profound level.

Companies doing internet book sales did not say, "Stop technology. We want to sell books." Instead, they used technology to sell books, and anything else they could get their hands on.

Then they made books into technology and sold that. They were thinking profoundly to acquire insights on how to go with the emerging flow. In fact, they were among the elite because they paddled much faster than just going with the flow. Acting on their profound knowledge put them ahead of the pack.

Your thoughts:

Prepare to Win

Brilliant:

People who are deemed to be brilliant are thought to possess exceptional intelligence in the way they find similarities and construct meaning for themselves, where others see only miscellany. They can see meaning forwards and backwards, and along parallel lines. They have the ability to combine skills and thoughts, to develop talents, and to project their unique understandings.

They bridge across intellectual structures, connecting ideas in a way that other thoughtful people have not pursued. Like the end of a good detective story, those other thoughtful people find the breakthrough to be fascinating, and in hind-sight they see a definite trail of development and discovery, and sometimes irony.

Consider these two physical descriptions of brilliance and the extension of the descriptions to traits of individuals. A jewel reflects the brilliance of the light through the many facets, carefully placed for reflectivity. Before electricity became common in homes, glass crystals in the light fixtures helped bounce candle light around the room. The brilliance in a person can bounce ideas off of lots of places in their brain to come up with sparkle and flash. Some of the ideas generated produce an increased perception of a truth, or a variation on a practice, or a fine tuning to a device, or perhaps even some innovation coming from a negative direction.

Other ideas flash with new light in areas of darkness: medical breakthroughs, artistic and architectural style, philosophy or theology reorganization, and most important of all, the "turning point" in the development of the life of each significant individual.

The other physical expression of brilliance is in appreciation of the qualities of acoustics, or music. If there is brilliance present, then the tone of an instrument will be reproduced so clearly that the actual instrument might as well have been present. It is a faithful recreation of the physical expression in the original. A brilliant reproduction of a performance is one where observers are moved as if the original were present. It represents a faithful presentation, a true projection, an authentic representation. There is a sense of perceiving perfection.

Brilliance can be noted in an astoundingly convincing transformative innovation of tremendous significance.

Combining the two metaphors, brilliance has the sparkle and flash of new thought and the high fidelity of already perceived reality. For us, brilliance can be noted in an astoundingly convincing transformative innovation of tremendous significance.

There are no brilliant people, but there are brilliant performances, brilliant literary works, brilliant scientific advances, brilliant social interventions, brilliant artistic products, and brilliant educational innovations. Some very impressive people speak on topics with brilliant insights. A correct boast can say that you were part of a group working on a project that turned out to be a brilliant event.

Prepare to Win

The same participants may at other times seem average, absent minded or even quite foolish.

Here are a few examples from school. Notices of Parent Club were leaving the classroom with the students but not reaching the parents. Using profound knowledge about students, it was noted that every child's coloring project ends up on the mom's refrigerator door. When that fact was taken into consideration, the fliers to moms were designed to double as coloring projects. Contact with parents improved.

In another situation, a kindergarten teacher was cleaning up a mess of red construction paper and paper lace debris while complaining that there were not enough Lego blocks on hand. Transposing something unremarkable to something of value, I took the pile of large but odd looking Valentine cards created by the kindergarteners to a local restaurant where they were sold for a dollar each from the wall at the cashier's station. The kids got new Lego's and the restaurant customers got a laugh.

There are thousands of new businesses waiting to be invented. New technologies will foster new entities. New combinations and applications of technologies will foster new enterprises. New ways to manage clumsy things, like academic planning, will sculpt new paths to think about ways to set up services and charities. All it takes to make these things take place is some brilliance.

Your brilliant insights may also come analogously, where you are able to imply parallel relationships in a new way. Innovations are adventures.

Prepare to Win

As you continue to read the chapters in this book, each one will conclude with comments about that topic's relevance to the terms Elite and Profound and Brilliant.

A part of being among the elite, and accomplishing profound work, will be based on your openness to doubt familiar paradigms, seek new concepts, aspire to more insight, partake in time for reflective thinking, metaphorically juxtapose layers of possibilities, rephrase, reformulate, reposition or rehearse what you know so that it becomes the base of your next level of learning. Thus, you will be polishing for brilliance.

The question of how far can you go is answered with the word "farther". John Dewey was an education philosopher who lived a hundred years ago. Among his many solid ideas about effective education is the concept of becoming a life-long learner. Dewey felt that every time you learn something, you were then ready to learn the information just beyond that. He thought that each person should start with practical knowledge and let it lead them into perpetual inquiry and learning. The initial fascination about the propulsion of a fire cracker in a can could lead a person into aeronautical engineering and rocket science.

So wherever you are, take your fascination to places no one has yet reached. Own the knowledge base that applies to your interest. And finally, manipulate your thinking to develop fascinating applications that the world has been waiting to see.

The higher standards are:

Elite. Profound. Brilliant.

Prepare to Win

Your thoughts:

Prepare to Win

"Three ultimate standards" from a biblical point of view.

Biblical issues that relate to these standards are many. Is it wrong to aspire to elite status? Remember that elite means to get there quickly, ahead of the others. Profound means to know your specialty thoroughly. Brilliant means to come up with significant and insightful new combinations and approaches. These are all elements of positive accomplishment.

The warning that goes with these standards is that your motivation can be wrong. If getting there first means that you do deliberate damage to others, running rough-shod over them, then they cannot respect you and your testimony is useless with them. That hyper-competitive behavior is probably due to either pride or greed.

The positive side of pushing for these three standards is the motivation of wanting to find new ways to rush a new medicine, with quality assurance about it, to the people languishing in misery without it.

Insights can come from anywhere. Indeed, God may guide you to a new idea. I bought a Scientific American magazine in an airport. An article described attempts by scientists to get an energy measurement of a sub-atomic particle that flickered between matter and energy so quickly, that the energy reading could not happen fast enough to get a magnitude measurement.

Then I thought, well, angels do that, too. They appear, do their thing, and then disappear. Perhaps they are just as real in their energy state as in their physical matter state. We convert matter to energy when we burn wood. Why couldn't God control energy states to accomplish his purposes too? And if He can, then when

Prepare to Win

the end of the world is supposed to include burning up the earth, a supposedly non-combustible object, all God has to do is to say, what was matter is now energy, and presto, heat and light take the place of matter. And that is what is described as burning. That's not so far-fetched, after all.

It also means that the soul might not be made of matter and would survive even that cataclysmic event. Making sense of that would add to God's credibility. But if this conjecture is entirely wrong, at least it made an interesting meditation. At least it takes God seriously. Brilliance accepts these ponderings as good practice.

In terms of effort and determination, Paul uses the analogy of a runner, pushing ahead. Paul said he put aside all encumbrances in order to run the race set before him. We are to always strive to achieve, even if it is just competing with ourselves for our personal best yet result (I Corinthians 9:24).

In terms of boldness versus timidity, consider Paul's words to a much younger Timothy, who he put in charge of a church group. Paul did not gradually build up Timothy's courage by saying lots of nice things about the boy. Paul told Timothy to take courage. Paul reminded Timothy that we are not supposed to be fearful. God has installed within us a spirit of courage. He has given us power to do great things in His name. He has given us the ability to love by faith, even when it is not reciprocated. He has given us the ability to live above circumstance and to think things through with sound reasoning (II Timothy, 1:7).

When someone in authority orders you to take courage like that, you do not have permission to hold back and wait for an invitation

Prepare to Win

or a sales pitch. A soldier is never asked, "If you think you can muster up some courage any time soon, would you mind fighting your way up that hill?" Of course not. Your challenge is to just step out in faith, obediently, and see what God wants to do with the situation.

God called Moses to go get the Children of Israel out of Egypt. Moses gave excuses about why he was a poor choice. God kept over-riding the excuses and finally Moses did as he was told (Exodus 3 and 4).

It is not dangerous to obey God. It may be difficult at times to perceive his will, but it is not dangerous to act on it when you feel certain about it. So take courage and move ahead as soon as you feel clear. Later, if it seems that you misunderstood God, He will allow you to re-organize and re-invigorate.

If you lose money by doing what you mistakenly believe is God's will, at least you will have obedience in your bank account. Timid people usually have little prominence, little wealth and little obedience in their bank accounts. The timid generally do not have credible witnessing power with influential people, either.

But when influential people follow your lead in your career, you may be able to lead them also to a significant faith also. For example, there is a Christian Embassy in Washington, D.C. where the staff works with government officials and foreign diplomats (among the elite). Many of the government workers have commented on their need to see more longterm (profound) results from their lives. These embassy workers patiently strive to find ways (brilliant) to lead others to stronger lives of faith.

Prepare to Win

Your thoughts:

Prepare to Win

Prepare to Win

Chapter 2: Purpose at Your Heart

Identify your personal philosophy by articulating your tenets of belief, your purpose, your non-negotiables, your passions, your individual skills, and your level of commitment. In other words, who are you and why are you here? And when you know that, ask about the level of your aspiration in that respect, like: Are you just good at math or are you a master manipulator of mathematical measures? Are you a construction worker or do you build cathedrals?

The first step in focusing is to articulate your tenets of belief. You are living a limited number of days. You are trading the time you could be on a beach for a more important purpose. What is it about your purpose that merits such a sacrifice?

Identify four areas where you are absolutely certain about what you believe. For example, Johnson and Johnson had a belief statement, a tenet, that they are a mom's best friend, so when the Tylenol scare happened, the company did not hesitate to take their product off the store shelves, making it unavailable to the mothers, until the product was cleared of suspicion in that particular case, and was once again certified as safe.

Prepare to Win

A belief statement for an educator may be: There is always more to learn beyond every lesson's conclusion. A tenet of belief for an attorney may be: Every client deserves his/her day in court. Perhaps an actor might say that no matter what happens, the show must go on.

What are the things that you believe so intently that no one can talk you out of them? What will you cling to when a crisis or a challenge pushes you to a tough decision? To what extent will you protect or provide for your family? To what length will you go to support human dignity? What will keep you from caving in to political pressure? When is enough, enough for you? What do you most want in your obituary or to be carved on your headstone?

Stop now and write at least four beliefs that you hold sacred:

1)

2)

3)

4)

As a reflective thinker, you will certainly return and revise or replace these statements. However, having these statements gives you an immovable base. It constitutes part of your personal character. It acts as the anchor so that you do not drift from your moral imperatives. It is the filter through which only some purified ideas may pass.

Write your purpose statement

You need a purpose statement to justify your existence. Why are you walking on this earth? What is the most important thing for you to accomplish? This statement will be very general. Here are some examples other people may have used.

*I want to be a source of encouragement and challenge to school children.

*I want to provide financial resources that will provide a significant amount of funding for breast cancer research.

*I want to show my children that a person can keep on learning and keep on serving those around them at any age.

*I want to safe-guard the jobs of hundreds of people by managing the company the best that I can.

*I want to preach to my congregation in such a way that they will dare to aspire to new and broader ways to be a blessing to others.

As of now, what would you say is your purpose? Write down some ideas of what you would like to accomplish:

Purpose Statement vs. Vision Statement vs. Mission Statement vs. Goal Statement

The Purpose Statement is a declaration of a life goal. A vision statement is a description of context for your ultimate purpose. This is what you measure other decisions by. What do you want to accomplish, generally. Are you here to advance theoretical physics? Do you want to make a life contribution to animal hospice activities? Perhaps you want to have the largest worm castings company in the world.

What kind of purpose statement could you come up with right now?

Coming up with a viable vision statement is the next challenge. A vision statement is not supposed to be attainable. It indicates your direction, like a guiding star. If you are the president of a small university, your vision statement may be that "The University will be prominent as an example of academic excellence coupled with societal interventions such that all of our students are abundantly equipped and publicly recognizable as a citizenry of enlightened benevolence." Now as you administer the university, support only those innovations that can make that vision more real.

How about setting vision goals like these: "People in my market will think of me first to see great culinary innovation." "I will surprise my prospective customers with my ability to innovate trend-setting design." "Those who come to me for counsel will

Prepare to Win

remark about my incredible insight and logical explanations." "People will appreciate my resilient character as I rebound and become a success once again." "I will fill my sermons with so much practical encouragement that members of my congregation will bring friends to church to hear the good news." "When people are in a difficult situation they will think of me first and they will call on me to provide statesman-like negotiation." "By offering more help than my team asks for, I will be known for my magnanimous collegiality."

When you succeed in articulating why your enterprise exists, and what it is that you want to see happen, your vision, you are clearer about your business concept, and you are more ready to launch the effort. Your co-workers or employees then have a clearer understanding, too, about what you are expecting, and that makes them less likely to make unfortunate assumptions. You will be able to say, "I know that you are doing it right when it looks like this."

If you are an inward thinker, close your eyes and look for vivid details of what your goal will look like. If you are an outward thinker you may have to get a friend to dialog with you in order to clarify what you want to see more clearly. If you don't know how to express your ideas, others will be wasting time as they wait for more direction, or they will accomplish their own interpretation of the goal, instead of what you want to see.

If you have already written your purpose statement, take time now to write your "pie in the sky" vision statement:

Prepare to Win

A Mission Statement is an expression of a short term project goal. When an Air Force pilot flies a mission, the pilot knows where he is going and what needs to be accomplished. By establishing a Purpose Statement, and a Vision Statement, each mission statement can be checked to make sure it conforms to the overall purpose and contributes to actualizing the Vision Statement. The Goal Statement indicates what measurements the mission needs to accomplish to be successful.

It is important to note that as missions become more short range, they increase in detail. Mission statements may be as simple as "today I am going to survey my customer service employees regarding their level of job satisfaction." The goal statement added is that "each employee will perceive that their satisfaction is important to me and to the company and, over time, there will be a resulting increase score in the survey of employee satisfaction."

A very important benefit of specific description is that you will be able to determine whether you have accomplished the goal, if you make sure that it is both detailed and measurable.

Take a moment to write a mission statement and an accompanying goal statement for a project that is common in your work life.

Prepare to Win

Is it still difficult for you to develop these statements? Perhaps more information is needed. You may not yet be at level of profound knowledge on that precise topic.

Do not be hurried. You need to find time to do reflective thinking. Try leaving the home or office and go for a walk and talk to yourself if you have to. If no one will walk with you, go by yourself and record any insights, so you do not lose any gems of wisdom among the sidewalk cracks.

You do not have to do this alone. Do you need a collaborative group to participate in the process? Will a brain-storming session help? Is there an expert you can consult?

To really wrestle with some issues, you may need to bring in others who think differently than your team does. Often an external facilitator can break through "group think" by challenging all of you. You may not always enjoy it, but you do need contrary thinking to test your ideas or to change your mind. Yes-men are a waste of space.

If you have several people available to address projects, and you can sort your employees into work groups, you may find it useful to assign divergent personality types to each group in order to achieve more diverse thinking. You may need someone quirky and creative to lead the charge in brainstorming. A quality controller is a person who calls the group back to the question at hand when the creative types get carried away down some distant road. A process manager will remind the group of the time constraints, budgets, and progress toward meeting the assigned outcome. Finally, a social initiator will keep encouraging the team and keep the feeling tone positive.

When you think about your work group, who would you classify into these personality based work styles:

Creative thinkers:

Quality control:

General project management:

Team encouragers:

Prepare to Win

Most people think that if they do what seems natural, everything will work out. Later, when they have not accomplished much, it is impossible to identify where they went wrong, because little of their attempt was specifically intentional. There are not many people who have thought through all these levels of intention.

If you have been intentional, if you have developed these layers of statements, you are among the **elite** in that respect. It may seem like you are slowing down the process, but the focus that results will produce great economies and propel your group.

Your industry trends and the particular collection of talent that you have available form a unique match. If you have taken care to work through these goals with a thorough knowledge of your organization and your industry, the clarity of your intentions are of a **profound** dimension.

If you discover ways to align these well articulated purposes so that they consolidate efforts, or if you can extend and broaden the goals to launch new initiatives, you are working the the field of **brilliance**.

Prepare to Win

"Purpose at your heart" from a biblical point of view.

Purpose: *"For God so loved the world*   motivation

Vision: *that he gave his only Son*   solution

Mission: *to die on Calvary's tree*   action

Goal: *from sin to set me free."*   achievement

The people in the Old Testament provide ample proof that if you follow God's purpose for your life, you will be blessed. On the other hand, if you stray from what God wants, a Babylon type experience is probably in your future. However, even then, when God's people were in captivity and Jerusalem was destroyed, there was reassurance from God that they would one day return and rebuild Jerusalem.

The metaphor of captivity in Babylon can represent many things: drug dependency, lost opportunity to mold the character of your children as they grow up, questionable business strategies that ruin your chances to be a viable political candidate, or other issues that may block your opportunity to fulfill some righteous purpose. Babylon--you do not want to go there.

You probably know of someone prominent whose indiscretion forced them to leave a religious, educational or political position of leadership. We have sinned and fallen short of the glory of God (Romans 3:23). The issue is that great responsibility requires

Prepare to Win

consistent accountability. That is the basis of trust. And we are all vulnerable. Elite status is not permanent, but can be maintained.

One of the ways that leadership is tested is by how long the leader has been living in a way that is consistent with the position held. That's why new believers and young people should be followers during a time of personal development. Temptations actually are opportunities to choose between good and evil. With each choice, God has provided a way of escape, if you take it (I Corinthians 10:15). But people are frail and do not always choose well.

If you are using a sound mind, you can choose to do what will ultimately contribute to your primary purpose. Studying the Bible and learning from other wiser individuals will help to establish a sound mind. As you mature in understanding who you are in God's eyes, and as you understand where you are still needing to learn to respond correctly, your good decisions will be more consistent.

Consider the dilemma faced by many teenaged girls. The pressure to have sex with a boyfriend is sometimes very strong. If the girl has a strong self-image, and if she is clear about her purpose in life and perceives how her purpose will be hindered by an untimely pregnancy, she has strength to do what is best for her. Armed with that ethical position, she may be able to see that sexual activity will not be in her best interest, and therefore she will have more reason to resist it.

Purpose, ethics and values are subjective. They are elements of preference. They are issues of choice, not right or wrong facts. You may oppose the ethical position of someone else, but ethics are presuppositions and opinions and have validity for the person holding them. That is why people say that you can never do any good arguing about politics or religion.

That warning is not entirely true. If it were true, there would be no reason to do evangelism. When you have an "Aha" experience, it means either that you have discovered new information, or that you have altered the way you see information and you have changed your ethical view. People can change political and religious positions, but by persuasion, not by proof alone. You cannot argue someone into Heaven.

People who believe in luck believe that there is an irrational likelihood of certain events happening in their favor and they are willing to bet their assets, sometimes hundreds or thousands of dollars, on that luck. They know that they don't deserve it any more than you do. Their ethical system includes the assumption that there is a flow of good vibrations headed their way and they need to catch the wave. "What goes around, comes around."

These same people who bet on an unseen irrational wave of fortune, reject the rational possibility that God's divine grace could be available to their life. They will bet on an unseen wave, but are unwilling to bet their assets on God's evident grace. How about you?

For the Christian, there is an assumption that blessings supernal are already granted, already flowing, and eternally bestowed. If Jesus died and rose again from the dead, demonstrating the believer's victory over the concept of the finality of death, then no better fortune can be granted. Your soul will never die.

Prepare to Win

When you add the relief from guilt that forgiveness offers (I John 2:1), and the promise that the steps of a righteous man are established by the Lord (Proverbs 16:9), and the assurance that God's unquenchable love extends even to your rebellious teenager (II Chronicles 7:3), you have much more security than someone who thinks their wave of luck might hold a little longer.

That is why you, as a believer, have the freedom to choose a purpose statement that is altruistic. You can aspire to the nobler things in life. When you are assured that God will meet your survival needs, you are free to meet God's expectation of service. Furthermore, as you are assured that God can establish your steps, you can engage wholeheartedly into the endeavor you perceive is His will for your life.

So do not pray for God to be with you (Matthew 28:20), which as a believer you already have. Instead pray that you will be granted enough insight to perceive His leading, to recognize His purpose for your life, and to appropriately use His blessings, in service to those around you.

People who know their purpose are grounded. As they mature, their behaviors increase in consistency. As time goes on, they find others to help support their ability to stay within the path of their value system. A good place to start to find support is in an active church fellowship.

Purpose *to work toward your* **vision** *so that each* **mission** *achieves the* **goals** *that promote glory to God.*

Prepare to Win

Your thoughts:

Chapter 3: Setting Smarter Goals

To establish smarter goals you need to move away from setting the hoped for quantity goals to planning the controlled quality goals.

Too often goal statements are dream statements like "I hope to increase my sales each year for the next ten years." There is too much that can happen during the next year that will probably send that goal off track. Your goal should be about what you can control, not what you hope. Otherwise, when a goal is unmet, there is always an excuse. You do not have to take any personal responsibility for coming short of your goal outcome when something beyond your control clearly is the reason the goal was not met. The only possible accusation in that scenario is that you did not hope correctly.

This book is about achieving great goals. But the word goal is just a generic noun. Too many people fall into the pattern of quantifying their goals, like "next year I will sell twice as many units as this year." If you are still determined to set quantity goals, why not at least set each quantity goal with a corresponding personal development goal or a personal effort goal?

Rather than setting a goal to sell twice as many units, how about setting a goal of reading or training to be more perceptive of the needs of your customers so that their transaction happens more quickly and more completely benefits them? Making better fits would probably result in more sales. As you look for better fits, you may even find yourself developing new markets.

What areas of personal development or professional skill development could you set as your priority goals today? How many additional customers will you see, if it is a matter of numbers and effort? How will you prequalify prospects if time cannot be stretched? Chances are good that as you increase the number of presentations you make, and the quality of the fit for your customer, your percentage of sales will also increase. Both increases together will multiply your earnings.

Instead of quantitative goal setting, make qualitative goals. What will you do to increase sales? "I will read five books on improved sales presentations over the next five months." "I will become a faithful member of a service-club and extend my network of contacts." "I will delay recreation activities until I have made sure each of my children has had personal time with me." "I will re-motivate myself whenever I need to by rephrasing what I do as it relates to my ultimate purpose in life." "I will develop the ability to recall names and faces."

How many books or seminars have you been through in the last six months to improve your contribution to the organization?

Prepare to Win

Write down some ideas of what you can do to develop your skills and increase your efforts, and then prioritize them:

In the sales arena, the quantity of your return is determined by your efforts and insights and by the economy, not just by your goal statement. The portion of your share of the market is probably more directly determined by your qualities and skills. Compete for whatever the market size is that is available. If you can grow your percentage of your field in the current economy, as the economy grows, your base grows right along with your expanding percentage of closes. That is an exponential increase.

Are you concerned about competition? Competition can be good as long as it enables you to shine by comparison. In fact, some entrepreneurs deliberately set up shop across the street from a weak competitor. Some executives try to get hired to replace a weak administrator because any improvement looks good. The task is to at least outshine the last guy.

Describe the type and strength of your primary competitors.

What features enable you to outshine your competitors?

Prepare to Win

How do you make the difference obvious?

The other part of setting goals has to do with time. When does work on a particular goal begin? What benchmark checks are scheduled? What is the projected end point for the project?

When you answer these questions and the sub-sets for each item, you have a flow chart. Usually it is a good idea to post it on the wall so that you can be aware and monitor whether reality matches the plan. Some activities may overlap; others must be completed in order to move on to the next. Your goals must include meeting both sequential and recurring time targets.

If you are deliberate about developing these statements, the focus you develop will save you both time and money. The sooner you establish the focus of your vision, the sooner you move out among the leaders, the **elite**. The more thoughtful and consistent your goal statements are, the more **profound** your efforts will be as they build upon each other, both deeper in understanding and higher in extending the applications. The more adaptable and innovative the goal accomplishments become, the more **brilliant** your pathway will seem. Bold leaders are people who are highly principled, able to proficiently articulate what they need to accomplish and who function consistently in the direction of their focused goal. They are the individuals found among the **elite** and **profound** and **brilliant**.

Prepare to Win

"Setting Smarter Goals" from a biblical point of view:

Is it humble to dream big dreams? How big is God? When Bill Bright started Campus Crusade for Christ with a handful of students at UCLA in the early 1950s, his goal was "to fulfill the Great Commission in this generation". He launched a movement on college campuses to do personal evangelism. Eventually the number of staff involved in Campus Crusade for Christ numbered many thousands.

*His leadership put him among the **elite** in that work. As he shared the Gospel over and over with students in private conversations and in fraternity house dinner presentations, he developed a **profound** familiarity with what succinctly needed to be said. That was profound knowledge of his audience's need. The **brilliant** thing that developed was a four point presentation, in a booklet, that anyone could use for an evangelistic conversation, The Four Spiritual Laws. (A copy is provided in this book, after the Epilog.)*

In addition to continuing the university campus ministry, his ministry eventually diversified into specialties in sports, musical ensembles, church training programs, the Jesus Film division, and expanded into almost every country in the world. Now there is even an on-line form of ministry. He dreamed big.

Billy Graham dreamed big. He went from tent preaching to football stadium preaching, and ministered around the world. He was called on by many U.S. presidents for counsel.

Prepare to Win

When the Bible tells us to not think more highly of ourselves than we ought to think, it is not saying to have minimal hopes. The context requires you to have sound judgement according to your faith. Every one of us needs to depend on God to participate in every meaningful endeavor, and to persist toward accomplishment.

What is the very biggest thing you think God could do through you? The context calls into play participation of your fellow believers and their endowments with spiritual gifts, the ability to perform in certain ways with divine aid. Do you have the faith to trust Him for just a little more than your casual expectation? What would that "little more" look like? Who else would be included?

There is something in the human nature that wants to command supernatural power. People pay a witch-doctor to cast a spell on someone. Or they go to a palm reader to find out more about the future than God has seen fit to reveal so far. Taking power that is reserved for God is challenging His authority (Malachi 3:5). A challenge like that did not do the Devil any good (Matthew 25:41).

Affirmations and chants do not command supernatural powers. A man once told me to say that a parking space would be open right where I needed it, and just speaking that phrase would make it come true. It was not a prayer. There was no "nevertheless thy will be done" clause. God was irrelevant to that man, and there was no good parking place when we got there!

Prepare to Win

When God works toward your goal it is because grace is at work and the end result should be glory to God, not to you. Your reward is the honor of participating in a special work. It is about what He does, not what you do. You are the servant, and He is the Master.

The guests at the wedding in Cana got to drink the best wine which was miraculously made by Jesus. That was very special for them (John 2:1). But the front row seats at the miracle went to the servants who did what Jesus commanded. If miracles are going to occur, wouldn't you like front row seats? Serve.

Your goals must never become more important to you than God's will. He is loving and just, so His will should certainly be good enough. But your goals are ways to demonstrate to others around you that faith works, and prayers get answered. You cannot out think what God can do, so ask boldly (Ephesians 3:20).

Prepare to Win

Your thoughts:

Chapter 4: Articulating Focused Roles

Accountability is the inspection of accomplishment in managing a task where both authority and responsibility have been assigned. In order to hold someone accountable, they must have been given enough authority or resources to accomplish the goal, and they must have been given sufficient direction to know how their work is to be measured.

Traditionally, accountability has been determined by the formal job description and the measurements were stated in the standards of performance. The job description tells the scope of the job. It addresses the various areas of responsibility that will be assigned to the employee. It also frequently lists who the job holder reports to and who reports to this position. The job description generally explains the role to be played by the employee.

The standards of performance, on the other hand, refer to the performance of duties assigned by the job description. In most cases the standards of performance include formal expectations, such as attendance at meetings with the vertical co-workers, as well as meetings representing the organization to outside interests. There may be a list of stipulated reports to be accomplished by

Prepare to Win

certain dates, or a list of reports to be completed whenever a situation requires description.

The job description and standards of performance are useful for new employees who need to make sure the major obligations are covered in a timely manner. They are also useful for seasoned employees to avoid being fired for lack of accomplishment. Work according to these expectations may be sufficient to keep the work unit active, but they are not sufficient to generate the kind of work leading to contributions that are elite, profound or brilliant.

School district boards establish Board Policies (BP) for the general purpose they want to see accomplished. Each policy should be followed by Administrative Procedures (AP), which explain how the policy is to be carried out or accomplished. In most cases, this requires hundreds of pages in board members' manuals.

Those documents address competence but they lack vision. They lack ambition. They lack passion. You do not have to love your organization to be devoted to doing significant work. You do, however, have to exert leadership to perform competently.

First, figure out your priorities. This is easy if you replaced someone who did the job poorly. It is quite likely that the thing that got that person fired is the first thing for you to do right. As you hone your priority list, check with others in your sphere of activity. In particular, check with the older secretaries. They are often the informal historians, and they also like to be included in significant discussions.

Next, put your intentions into words. Describe your priorities and how you think they should be accomplished. Couch your ideas

Prepare to Win

with descriptive language, using carefully selected adjectives and adverbs. Frame your thoughts within the context of the job site. Make it robust because it is a large part of your life, and you want your life to be robust!

If you think it does not sound too audacious, share these thoughts with your boss. The feedback will give you a reality check. It may give the boss a new look at your perspectives. It will probably make you stand out among so many other less articulate employees.

Be articulate and respectful of your employees. They deserve to know exactly what their roles are in supporting your role. Your work in developing these clarifications about expectations are a big part of establishing your style of corporate culture.

Then how will you play your role in the organization? Master collaborator? Lone genius? Fearless forager? Fount of inspiration? Hopefully, you won't be seen as just another workaholic.

Others will not object to your prominence, if you let them ride along on your coattails. If you leave all the others behind in a cloud of institutional dust, you may see them again in an ambush just around the implementation corner.

Transparency is when others, co-workers or constituents, have access to accountability data. As technology causes more people to have access to information, there is an increase in the expectation that germane data is open to inspection. This mitigates against suspicion.

Prepare to Win

That leads to one last comment about failure. You may want to check on your organization's tolerance for failure. Things don't always work out and in some cases, heads will roll. Each boss has an opportunity to decide whether a failure is part of doing business or if it is an organizational learning opportunity. Depending on the state of the economy, the scale of a failure will be an issue.

Never leave a job on a low point. If you get to stay, then stay there. After you accomplish a big win, you may be able to parley that into a bigger job somewhere else, or even a promotion rather than departure where you are. Only change employment on a win.

What approach has not been done there that will make your work stand out (**elite**)?

What is there about the priority list that needs more research or experimentation or a pilot project (**profound**)?

How can you combine culturally acceptable practices of your organization with your unique insight to bring about a new twist (**brilliant**)?

Prepare to Win

"Focusing Articulate Roles" from a biblical point of view.

Job description for a believer: disciple all nations.

Standards of performance: baptizing and teaching.

When you take on a project at church, make sure you know exactly what you are expected to do and when it should be done. Be just as precise when you recruit others to assist you. Using the word recruit was a deliberate choice. Churches too often ask for volunteers and few show up. Jesus recruited the disciples. People respond to a challenge when the vision is gripping.

People who raise money for building projects or scholarship funds know that they have to find individuals with money and they have to make bold requests for large donations, and of course, those donors often give.

If your project is important to God, he will supply the resources. You have to seek. He will provide. Ask. You cannot be sure how God will work in the heart of another person unless you ask them.

That does not mean that you do not need a sales pitch. People need to know what they are being asked for. They can respond much better, positively or negatively, to clarity than to fog.

As you work to gather resources, your faith will grow as God provides. Faith builds on experience. You may resist the job of raising support for a project, but then, when you do it, the results will build your faith. How can you grow without getting experience with God, and how can you get experience without engaging with a big challenge?

Just like approaching someone to talk about Jesus takes courage, approaching others for any spiritual reason takes a determination that you want to see the goal accomplished. Remember that you are not alone, without spiritual oversight.

Ego protection is a luxury that a believer cannot harbor. When a stranger rejects what you kindly say, they are not rejecting you. They do not even know you. If you feel bad, it should only be because you wish the other person had understood better what was being offered.

When I worked with an evangelistic organization in Sweden, I went to my boss and complained that it had taken several months before I had finally found someone willing to pray to accept Jesus, after sharing the Gospel with 155 university students. I felt that my work until that day was fruitless.

His response was that all I could do is share the Gospel. Anything that happened beyond that was God's responsibility. My role was being performed correctly, and that was enough. If I had given up after 55, there would have been another 100 students who would not have received the Good News.

Paul said that he planted, Apollos watered, but God gave the increase. Keep doing what you believe God wants you to do, but have others confirm that it is done well (I Corinthians 3:6).

Prepare to Win

Your thoughts:

Prepare to Win

Your thoughts:

Chapter 5: Lightning Decision Making

It is not necessary to take a long time in order to make a good decision. It is necessary to take a lot of trouble to make a good decision. That is why people often caution you to take your time. They believe that as time ticks by, you might think of another item that needs consideration. But if you are meticulous about a check list, you can move through a comprehensive list of items quickly, and still make a good decision.

Wouldn't you want your intensive care ward doctor to be both thorough and quick? Do you want the doctor to say, "Your treatment choice is an important decision. You are near death. I had better take a few days to make sure I have the right decision. In a couple of days I might think of something else that is important." Actually, nurses with checklists, following doctors around the intensive care unit, is a relatively recent development.

Do you remember your teacher telling you that a question well-stated is half answered? Make sure that the decision you think you have to make is really addressing the issue needing improvement. Then, take pains to state the need precisely.

Prepare to Win

Is a quality production problem a result of poor employee effort or poor employer training? Is the high school dropout rate the result of dysfunctional homes or is it due to the resistance of teachers to develop intervention strategies to salvage a student's future? Is poor communication due to a lack of newsletters or is it the result of under-valuing the potential recipients?

As you can see by these examples, a quick fix is a temporary fix. Deep issues keep popping up, so you might as well address them, as painful as that may be. When you feel that you are at the real cause of the situation you can directly address it.

Then study your topic. All good professional research begins with a survey of "the literature" on research others have accomplished on related issues. That means getting the most up-to-date information and it means being cautiously skeptical so that you don't act on someone else's faulty notions. It should put you at the front edge of knowledge (profound), ready to launch (brilliant), in order to be out there first (elite).

When you are clear about the topic, what are the results that you need? It is not enough to say you need a new car. What traits would best suit your situation: cargo area, number of seats, engine power, price range, fuel economy, color, warrantee, four wheel drive? If they are not equally important you can assign different weighted values to each criterion.

When you have your list of solution criteria, you can go shopping. Comparison between choices is essential when items do not clearly match your specifications. If gold trim was not on the list, but a salesperson says it denotes a special person, don't be swayed, and do not pay for it. It is not your fault it is on the car. Use your list.

When you drive home in the vehicle that best met all your weighted preferences, you can feel assured that you made a good decision. Making the decision did not take long, but it was done carefully. One of the keys to being among the **elite** is to act quickly, decisively, but carefully.

What decision is waiting for completion in your work? What is the real need?

What are the solution criteria that a good decision will need to satisfy?

What options can meet your real need and also satisfy your solution criteria?

Which solution seems like the easiest to implement, most affordable, best company-cultural fit?

By limiting your shopping to a narrow array of criteria, and becoming an expert just on those, you developed a **profound** but limited knowledge base for decision making.

Prepare to Win

People who have a reputation for acting both quickly and wisely in finding and compounding great solutions and are often considered **brilliant**.

Prepare to Win

"Lightning decision making" from a biblical perspective.

What about the hard decisions? Assume that you are the manager of a bank. You want everyone to know that you are a Christian by your love. Two employees are chronically late and sometimes are rude to customers, even though you have documented conversations about that with them on several occasions. One is a believer and the other is not.

You may think that if you fire the non-believer you may cause them to resent Christians and they may die without Christ. If you fire the believer they may tell all your church friends and their coworkers that you are a jerk, and not the mature Christian you have claimed to be. Yet, your vice president has instructed you to remove them now.

Daniel showed us that we are to obey those in authority over us unless the ethical issue is worth walking into a fiery furnace (Daniel 3). So these employees have to go. That is for sure. The organization will not function well unless you do the deed.

God will find other ways to accomplish his will. You are not big enough to block God's ability to find other ways to accomplish His goals with those people. Maybe getting fired will make them get serious about their lives.

Have you ever heard that you cannot please all the people all of the time? That is not in the Bible, but there are plenty of examples in the Bible of displeasure by one faction or another. Your witness includes doing your job well. It is just a fact that slander and resentments are sin litter in the interpersonal world we live in.

You have demonstrated that you are a person with compassion, so let the dismissal conversation be objective and gracious. People feel that there is a greater sense of justice when they have a chance to speak up and respond to what is happening to them. You will probably have to be the one to end the conversation, though.

Remember that anyone can be the good guy and hire people. It is a mark of a real leader to be able to end someone's employment. This is not because it is a fun thing to do, but because to make an organization functional, a badge of courage goes to the person who can force the change that is needed.

These paragraphs were about your behavior. The behavior of those employees is beyond your control. The non-believer may see that you had good reasons. Or they may have to be reached through the ministry of someone else. God can still call them to faith. You are not the only tool in the shed.

The believer who is resentful has some spiritual maturing to do. This experience will probably add to the maturation process. That there are people who misunderstand what has happened is just a fact. Consider how many people believe the lies political groups promote. The truth is not always obvious to everyone. The world is imperfect. In fact, none of us are perfect, either.

Prepare to Win

Your thoughts:

Prepare to Win

Your thoughts:

Chapter 6: Service is the Product

Customers always like getting big portions.

Make the act of giving service to others be your most important contribution in life. That does not mean that you are selling everything you own and that you are becoming a slave to others. It means that you exist to provide a benefit to others. They are not just customers with money in their pockets: money that you want. They are beneficiaries of your input. They should perceive that they are better off having been with you.

Your beneficiaries will gladly pay for getting benefits that you provide to them, and you in turn will make sure they get heaps of benefits for their money.

What are the most important benefits that people need? Maslow was a psychology professor. He felt that individuals primarily need physical survival and safety, followed by beneficial human interactions, and with all of that accomplished, he thought that people become that authentic, unique and selfless individual that they are capable of becoming.

Prepare to Win

So in the way you do your serving of others, the first level that people need is sufficiency in physical and safety issues. Do you sell durable clothes? Can you provide reliable transportation? Are there ways you can help protect the things your customers hold precious? Is there a housing issue that you can expedite? Can you help safeguard their future assets? Will their children have a better future with your teaching or your medical care? Can you serve them abundantly there?

Or, going beyond that, what can you do to enhance their interpersonal interactions? Can you provide counsel, direction, instruction, encouragement, entertainment, relaxation, or even solace? Are they glad you came into their life?

What are the services you can provide to your customers? Can you serve them quickly?

How can you provide excellence in serving them? Do you have quality assurance roles in your business?

Do you have a way to tailor your service to best fit each one? How does someone make brilliant changes to the profound basic service so that your customers feel like you exist just for them?

Do you ask them for evaluations and suggestions? How do you consider that feedback? Big corporations use focus groups to get objective information about their products. Sales figures alone are not enough to tell you how your product is valued. Innovation is often a response to issues raised about an item.

Do you ask your clientele for referrals and testimonials? Referrals help to open doors by providing you with the credibility of the person referring you. Testimonials provide a service of helping other customers envision their own satisfaction with what you offer. How have you made referrals and testimonials work for you?

Being the first one to show up with just the help they needed makes you among the **elite**. Being there with the quality of understanding and service that exactly matches the needs makes you **profound**. Finding solutions to the crisis which has blinded them with urgency, makes you **brilliant**.

Prepare to Win

"Service as the product" from a biblical point of view.

The early church was good about doing service for others. Paul said that true and undefiled religion was shown by taking care of widows and orphans (James 1:27). The elderly were to be honored and cared for. Deacons were appointed to make sure the tables with food were taken care of, so that the elders could focus their work of service with a priority to pray and teach.

The Apostle Paul provided that kind of praying and teaching service at the cost of supporting himself with tent-making. Furthermore, he performed his service at the occasional expense of being beaten, jailed, and having to leave town through a window. Are you that dedicated?

Finally, are you generous with your service? A baker's dozen means that any purchase of 12 gets one more for free. Is that how you do service, with everyone getting a little more than they expected? Do they get more items, or quicker service, or better quality than they expected? These are all elements of having your master say that you have done well, and that you are a good and faithful servant (Matthew 25:21).

Prepare to Win

Your thoughts:

Prepare to Win

Your thoughts:

Chapter 7: Powerful Paradigmatic Proaction

The next crucial element in the adventure of living your life is the implementation plan. You have a purpose, and a vision, and a way of making decisions, and some ideas about how you will serve others. Now you need to establish specific steps in a plan, and then you have to follow the plan, pretty much. Having a plan invites action. Being observant will help you modify the plan as it is being implemented according to what elements seem to need some changing.

Industries have learned that they must be sensitive to the changing public they serve. Some companies go so far as to say that they have reinvented themselves every few years. But you cannot hesitate, intending to implement action when the next generation of needs takes form, because you will be at the end of the line, and not up among the elite. Get in now, and make necessary changes while you are engaged in doing what you do.

While it is essential that you have a vision and a plan, you must also be able to allow for some ambiguity as you puzzle out some solutions on the job.

Prepare to Win

If your vision is not clear enough, you will just dabble in the area of your interest.

If you do not have the financial base you need, you will be halting your momentum every time the cash flow stops.

If you do not have the technical training, you will be doing shoddy work.

If it is not clear who has what responsibility in your organization, gaps in service will appear.

If you do not have target dates for stages of development, you will never know if you are on schedule, and interest payments will eat your capital.

If you do not know your competition, you can only hope for customers, instead of winning them.

If you do not know who to form strategic alliances with, you will stand precariously alone in your endeavor.

If you are not honest, considerate and consistent with your team, you will not enjoy their loyalty.

Leadership is a big job. You have to be multi-talented and you have to be ubiquitous. That means you have to be able to examine what you are supervising and you should seem to be everywhere that you need to be all the time. There's no time for procrastination.

You can't steer something that doesn't move.

Prepare to Win

Procrastination is not usually a result of laziness. It is more likely to be a result of anxiety about getting into the process or about handling the result. When you complete your degree, you'll have to compete for higher level employment positions, and like the competition in classes, there will be competition with a new, higher level of peers at the new employment. As you start working there you will feel clumsy and foreign, but that's normal. So did each of your co-workers.

Those new peers are already functioning there, and you are the new person trying to get in step with the rest. Soon you, too, will know where they keep the supply of paper clips. If you are concerned about being really able to swim with a new set of sharks, just take courage for the adventure and dive in anyway.

After all, if you have made it through the hiring door, you have the right to come in. The people you will be working with probably have had less formal training than you have. They will have more on the job training than you have, but that will come for you, too, with time. By the time you finish reading this book, you will know how to expedite the process of productivity.

Most people are working at a promotion level their boss realized was too high, but they never got fired because it was the boss who made the mistake of promoting them, and he does not want to admit it. Those people just never get another promotion, so there they sit. That's generally your worst case scenario, getting stuck too, so relax.

Deniers and delayers have stress that results from not dealing with anxiety. Some people deny that they put something off until later.

Prepare to Win

They are dishonest about their knowledge of the pending task. Others admit they know about it, but say that to get past the anxiety they need to first have a snack, watch some TV, get a drink or a smoke, resulting in poor health. Then they water the plants, walk the dog and feed the fish. By then the stress has been distracted and they figure another day of delay is no big deal. That life-style perpetuates, and the individual feels trapped.

But as a take-action figure, you will actually have less stress because your stress will come from interacting with your environment and things will get resolved, bringing a welcome end to the stress about that particular issue. The result may have been good or it may have been bad, but the issue is resolved. For that poor procrastinator, though, his stress is locked in place as long as the issue remains unresolved. Seek truth and light, and avoid darkness.

What things are you putting off today? Why are you fearful of attacking the issues?

Structure your life for habits of productivity. Instead of delaying the next task, proclaim that you are on top of the issue and that you are determined to energetically get moving with it. Determine that you don't have time for a snack, can't concentrate with the distraction of TV, need a clear head with sobriety, and get your kicks out of your own accomplishments, not from nicotine. Get into a business-like place in your home or office, and act like your future depends on it, because it does.

Demonstrate confidence even if you are acting.

Prepare to Win

You should act and dress for the success you aspire to. If you do computer programming, that's cool, man. But if you have a sales goal in a public company, spiff yourself up with a silk tie to go with your professional outfit. The purpose of this is more for your self-image than it is for making a positive impression on others.

If you have to walk for your activity, move with a confident, brisk stride. Start every conversation smiling. Acknowledge the presence of everyone around. Use good grammar and speak up so you don't have to repeat yourself. Demonstrate confidence even if you are acting. At lunch meetings, use good table manners. When you change your behaviors, your attitudes will follow.

It is often helpful to model yourself after a person who has the traits that you admire. As you visualize what they would do in a given context, you put flesh on the mannerisms that will serve your function best. Who knows, you may also be the model for someone else to emulate. It is said that emulation is the purest form of flattery.

One way to reduce the stress is to list the elements of the task at hand. As you carefully put together a list of tasks, you will discover that it is not a lurking ghostly creature, but a simple to-do list of things you can attack individually and accomplish promptly. Many employers have found it useful to meet with an employee who claims to have too many responsibilities and list all the job expectations. On paper the list has an undeniable objectivity. Then you will both objectively know the content of the task.

Here is the key to making things get done. Content and sequence are the two things that open your avenue to action. If you know what you need to do and you know how you need to do it, your way is clear. This is essential in addressing writer's block. Once research is sufficient, and the writing format is established, there is nothing left but to be productive.

The logical way to reduce procrastination stress and establish how you need to do the job is to prioritize the necessary tasks. Some items on that list may have to get some advance work, like applications or advice. But mostly, you can just work your way down the list. Do the most important thing first, move to the second, and so forth.

What if you cannot get to all the items on the list? This way you don't have to eliminate the non-productive things in your life. They just don't happen because higher priorities come first. Remember that content and sequence are the two things that open your avenue to action.

Is it hard to turn your back on activities that are poor uses of your time? Some time wasters are habitual or sentimental and it is difficult to dispose of them. You do not have to reject the unproductive things in your life, just neglect them. People working at an elite status are too busy for time-wasting interference, and it is acceptable to fondly say that you miss the old ways.

Some organizations have such a difficult time discontinuing the old ways that they have memorial services for them. The whole group gets together, reminisces about how things used to work so well under other conditions, and then they say good-bye because those ways don't work here anymore.

Prepare to Win

Action short circuits both initial stress and inertial anxiety: front-loading is the cure. Begin working just as soon as a previous stage is completed. Don't backwards plan from a deadline. Too many unpredictable issues can interfere with the schedule. Instead, think like a runner who always wants to beat the previous fastest time. How far ahead of schedule can you get the entire job done this time?

What are the first five things you will work on as soon as this reading time is over?

Celebrate the increments of accomplishment. Celebrations are like push-blocks on a track to push against for the next sprint. If you are taking courses toward a certificate, or a degree, celebrate each quiz and finished research paper. Celebrate the completion of each class. Celebrate each degree with a framed diploma displayed prominently where you will see it. Move some easy wins up front in the priority list just for the thrill of achieving them.

What will be the next celebration related to your work?

Significant corrections require deep introspections.

When you take action, try to address the root issues. Administrators spend a great deal of time fighting fires that flare up, and they have little time left to address the underlying issues that prove to be incendiary. Quick solutions are inserted in the employee handbook without reference to cultural components that may be in conflict and have to be addressed later. The key to discovering underlying issues is to look at the cultural context. The problems you see are probably symptoms of something deeper. Here are a couple of examples.

The constituents complain that there is poor communication and they want a web-site updated frequently, in addition to the standard newsletter. So the administrator has to divert scarce resources to create a digital place for the newsletter to be posted. But nothing improves.

The cultural issue in this case is a lack of regard for the potential recipients of the communication. If you don't care about them, you won't make the effort to get your information to them. If you do care, you would email them, call them, or even visit them. The lack of communication is really a lack of caring. The lack of caring about others effects the culture of the organization in many broad measures beyond newsletters. The cultural values are what you should work on.

Another example deals with the topic of bullying at school. Teachers and parents clamor for policies to punish bullies. They may even bully the administrator to get tough with bullies. The underlying issue, though, is that the school has not made the effort to structure a system for students to constructively address aggressive behavior of classmates and manage their conflicts. My doctoral dissertation was on the effectiveness of using democratic class meetings to resolve conflicts by empowering the class to confront the bully and the class assigns a logical consequence.

One reason for recidivism in prisons is because when we punish people. They get punished each time they get in trouble. If we correct people, they understand how to make better choices. While we may not be able to address character issues so deeply ingrained by the time they are adults, would it not be wise to establish a structure to teach students to make better choices in the school years? How can you be a good citizen if you cannot resolve your own interpersonal issues? (But it's not on the state test.)

What current problem are you working on? What is the underlying motivation for whatever is pushing the issue? Can you adjust the situation at a deeper level and ameliorate the symptom?

Principle Review: Elite and Profound and Brilliant

As you move out ahead of others, you do not have the time to procrastinate. Whatever stage of a project you are in, the due date is now if you want to be among the **elite**. No one ever got to the top of their game by never starting one.

As a **profound** thinker, you evacuate from your location of procrastination, to plunge deeply into the essential issues that have to be tackled. They may be vague initially, but intense concentration in the subject area will eventually gel into categories and priorities. In order to get brilliant thought to happen, you have to immerse yourself in the presence of every pertinent implication, application and all possibilities for variations and breakthroughs.

Then you have to find new implications, applications and expanded possibilities. There is no longer the opportunity for procrastination. Every issue demands that you get into it quickly, process it deeply, and **brilliantly** resolve it with the best of many possible solutions. Then you will be among the Elite and Profound and Brilliant.

Prepare to Win

"Powerful paradigmatic proaction" from a biblical point of view.

In the evangelical community there have been lots of paradigm shifts. Luther changed how people regarded church governance and foundational theological bases. He set spiritual words to common drinking songs. There may have been traditional people who preferred the chanting of church leaders, but the paradigm changed to hymns set to popular music. Does that struggle to shift paradigms sound familiar?

One hundred years ago churches were supposed to have pointed roofs and bell towers. These days, many new churches look more like office parks. Organs and pianos are replaced with worship bands. Church attenders are more likely to tap their feet to music than to get down for prayer on a kneeling bench.

The first thing to ask when faced with a paradigmatic shift is whether scripture takes issue with it. The second is whether the shift would actually fit the situation better. Then it is important to make sure that the implementation is done in a way that practices love.

Is it right for a church to divide between old people in a traditional service, separated from younger people in a contemporary service? Will the wisdom of a lifetime of faith touch lives in a younger part of the congregation? Will the energy of the younger people address the situation of the more frail of the senior saints?

The purpose of the church is to nurture and equip the saints. How does your fellowship nurture all members in an authentic way?

Prepare to Win

How does your fellowship equip all the saints for service in customized ways?

In what ways do all the participants in your church participate in redefining the evidence of unity, love and productivity?

Many ministries have unlimited potential. As a lay person in your church develops a ministry, and it grows beyond that person's ability to administer it, does the church, whose job is to equip the saints for all good works, have structures and resources to promote and advance the growth of that ministry, or is the church office only for supporting the ministry of the pastors? That is a paradigm question.

Prepare to Win

Your thoughts:

Prepare to Win

Your thoughts:

Chapter 8: Engineering Lasting Change

It is common practice to speak of change as a noun, but it is a verb. You cannot vote for change. You can only vote to change. Change is a process. You cannot point at change, but you can point at something that is changed. After all, that is the only thing they are selling you in the evening news: information on what has changed today.

In a way, change is like a remodeling project. You can't just wish it was different, or perform a trivial effort like altering it by painting it a different color. You have to make substantial physical alterations in a space to have a change called remodeling.

In terms of participating in a culture of perpetual change, the "under construction" sign is always somewhere in the organizational environment. The sooner your associates understand that, the sooner they will learn to function among some shifting areas of ambiguity. Remember, though, that ambiguity must be a place where vision is sharpening, a place with a clarifying purpose, not areas of neglect or confusion or mutiny. One of your goals is that you are always moving toward order, away from chaos.

Prepare to Win

Remodeling almost always requires deconstruction to some extent. It is unfortunate when, in the business sense, that includes laying off people in the organization who are no longer contributing to the evolving entity. It is doubly unfortunate when management replaces existing staff who could have been retrained to contribute to the advancing performance needs.

Change requires an imbalance between opposing powers. Things which are balanced do not move. Without social conflict there is no cultural improvement. If your company is doing well but not evolving to stay on the competitive edge, you may actually have to insert instability in order to remain relevant.

A peaceful organization is at homeostasis. Everything functions and no change happens. When you remove one or more supports, the organization scrambles to retain balance. That scramble will either re-install the missing supports or the scramble will be to develop an alternate solution, a change in the paradigm.

Businesses and families are not always balanced. The usual term for that condition is dysfunctional. They have already lost the struggle for balance and limp along, struggling to just survive at a lower, more basic level. Only radical therapy can improve them.

Take a moment to review the dynamics of paradigm shifting. A paradigm is an established understanding of how things are done. It is a protocol that has wide acceptance. There is a paradigm of how to dress for the opera. There is a paradigm of what constitutes conformity to a major political party. There is a paradigm of who does which chores in your own home.

Prepare to Win

Shifting to a different paradigm is often a source of new blood to an organization. Paradigms shift into space available; they do not create their own space. That is why packaged solutions, which need to retain their own space in order to be effective, do not always fit well.

The chief problem in shifting paradigms comes in the resistance to change. At first non-conformists are considered odd. As more join with them they are seen as trouble-makers. As even more join with them, they are seen as the progressives, and eventually with almost everyone on board they are regarded as the new "old guard".

A leader of change must have such a clear understanding of the vision for the new entity and a devotion to the non-negotiable tenets of belief, that this leader acts as a screener or a gatekeeper and allows only the development of structures consistent with the tenets and only the ones that lead in the direction of the vision. Maintaining the plan requires determination and diligence.

The culture for an effective change must embrace the new way of thinking. "That's how we do it here." The goal is for all the staff to use the same terminology so that discussions are accelerated and consensus in the new context becomes the expectation. Getting that common ground established takes lots of work and lots of conversation.

With every change there must be a realignment of the systems that operate within the organization. That is where the inter-personal annoyances come in. One thing impinges on another. When you change a family practice, like instituting family devotions, mixed motives, complicated schedules already in place, format and

Prepare to Win

guidance, as well as individual roles assigned are all issues that have to fit into a new system. Adjusting the change is work.

Suppose you decide to start the school day an hour earlier so that sports travel only cuts the last period. Or suppose you decide that teens need to start school an hour later because of their sleeping habits.

Either way, parents must be convinced so that they adjust the time for preparing to leave for school. The bus system has to change because other schools in the district may not want to be changing schedules in the same way. Teachers with children at home will now be leaving home to go to work at school at a different time and child care, either before or after school, will be altered.

There are other questions that will need to be answered. Will this still be a good idea when daylight savings time changes? Is there an increased safety hazard? Will the unions agree to the change in working conditions? Does state law interfere?

All of these complications are why change for change's sake is a waste of energy and emotion.

The quickest way to make change is to have exterior forces act upon your organization, so that resisters embrace change as the desperate attempt of the organization to continue to exist. If the force comes from someone within the organization, a paradigm switcher, saboteurs in the group will address that trouble-maker, and change will stop. Peace will return.

An example of internal resistance to change is where a political appointee is unable to alter practices by the employees in civil-service positions down the ladder. Or consider the newly arrived second lieutenant as he interacts with a battle experienced group of soldiers. The system in place takes precedence over leadership, unless the paradigm changes.

Consider political upheavals in various countries. When the mob in the streets accomplishes the removal of despotic rulers, the organization of authority is shattered and needs to be restored in some fashion, sometimes just like before but with different names, or it may be changed to provide more transparency and accountability to the public. Perhaps it will disintegrate into factions and neighborhood militia. Of course, this process is greatly affected by the free exchange of reliable information and by the cultural coalescence of the population. Cell phones and social media play an amazing new democratizing role in evolving people movements.

Closer to home, in California, the state legislature decided that primary students should be in classrooms of 20 students or less and the state had enough money to pay for it. Change was instantaneous.

However there were not enough classrooms for these additional teachers, so additional portable classrooms had to be financed by the state as well. And many teachers in high stress positions like special education acted on the negotiated contingency of lateral transfers into regular education classrooms of 20 or less students, so there was a sudden need for new special education teachers.

Changing to respond to that need, universities began issuing combined teaching credentials to include special education authorizations to meet the immediate need. Consequently, many of these new Resource Teachers were less resourceful than had been the case for that term previously.

Because change is a process, and ambiguity is its face, the leader must articulate a clear vision of purpose and product, as the organization formulates new expectations, routines and systems. Field tests and pilot projects help to provide others in the organization with an image of the emerging reality.

As job expectations are clarified, and hierarchy is established, the organization is poised once again, unfortunately, to languish in homeostasis, unless a heroic leader comes forward.

The next chapter talks about power and persuasion, but first take a moment to reflect on leadership style. "Heroic leaders" like World War II generals, industrial titans, movie moguls, all had the essence of self-sufficiency. They gave the orders and others obeyed.

For the last twenty or thirty years the "collaborative leader" has taken over, drawing on expertise in various strands, melding consensus, sharing the credit. The heroic leader was professionally limited but decisive. The collaborative leader achieves broader competency, but at the price of compromise and delay. Frankly, you have to be both, depending on the situation.

What would you change in your endeavor to create a new paradigm of expectations?

Prepare to Win

What would it take to establish better routines to accomplish your mission?

What systems are in place that have a vested interest in resisting your impetus?

Which of your business essentials will you defend heroically?

To be among the **elite** at the front of change, you and your associates must embrace opportunities for change. To make sure that all systems work in synchronization with the new culture, you have to ensure that there is a **profound** adoption of the change. Finally, you must make sure that the changes are **brilliant** and that your entity is like no other. Be the first to change, a group determined to make deep, smart change, and manage the process so that the way you do things are significantly changed.

Prepare to Win

"Engineering lasting change" from a biblical point of view.

Look at the big picture first. Change. Jesus said He did not come to change the Law, but to fulfill it. Yet, the work of our Lord undeniably changed history. He did away with the need for a physical offering on an altar by becoming our sin offering.

What changed from God's side?

- *God's righteousness was satisfied, in spite of our sin.*

- *Our sins were forgiven, even though, at the time, they were all in the future. Some of your sins are still in your future, but as you see, they have already been paid for.*

- *We were adopted into the family of God.*

- *We are benefactors of God's mercy, grace, blessings and spiritual fruits and spiritual gifts.*

- *Together, we the church, are described as having an intimate and protected relationship with Christ as a bride to a groom.*

- *We are assured that physical death is not terminal, but transitional.*

Those are some of the changes God has made on our behalf, without our help. That's a lot.

Prepare to Win

How should we respond to the change in our relationship to God?

- *Humbly, for we are the created and God is the creator.*

- *Gratefully, for forgiveness and blessings.*

- *Reverently, acknowledging the greatness of God.*

- *Obediently, recognizing that His direction for our lives must be the best thing for us.*

- *Trusting that God loves us and will care for us as we seek to please and glorify Him.*

- *Allowing our life practices and habits to change, conforming with His values, adding to His glory.*

- *Generously sharing with others their opportunity to establish an eternal relationship with God.*

Prepare to Win

Your thoughts:

Chapter 9: Conflict, Power and Politics

Power is the ability to get what you want from others. What you get may be compliant behaviors of service or votes, or it may be acquiring wealth in the form of commodities. Manipulation has its limits. You can force compliance, but you cannot force agreement. Agreement requires persuasion, not coercion.

Democracy is the free and diverse participation in decision making about the distribution of power. Politics is the negotiation of various forms of power: status, wealth, political influence, intimidation, intelligence.

One would like to think that negotiation is simply a matter of friendly persuasion and making trades on issues of minor relevance. However, negotiation may devolve into bullying, manipulation, aggressiveness, demands, fighting or extortion. People who have no institutional base of authority use intimidation to accomplish their purposes.

At the professional level, many legal battles rely on threats of litigation to accomplish a goal. In more informal places, some parents in poor neighborhoods have learned to protect themselves or their children's interests through tough assertive behaviors.

Prepare to Win

As a school principal I have had parents disagree with a student suspension from school. Their choice of words and emotional level were difficult to endure, but when they threatened to call the state governor, I always felt pity that they could not come up with a better threat than that.

(As parents stood at my office door yelling at me, telling me I was a terrible principal, I sat there, stone-faced, looking over their shoulder at a small print on the far wall behind them, of Einstein sticking his tongue out. Way to go, Einstein!)

Consider the playground bully who needs attention, or a sense of empowerment, or perhaps is just greedy for something someone else has. For many individuals it is easier to intimidate someone to get a goal than to charm someone to get the same goal, especially if you have to good-naturedly share it with the person who has it. But if you take something from someone else, you get it all. Bullies know what makes a better return on investment.

Bullies look for a weak person or weak spot. In the same way in a group situation, power seeks to fill a vacuum. If you have positional authority and you do not lead, others will occupy the position by default, although unofficially. If you call a meeting, they will control it. Collaboration can easily lead to co-optation as the interests of one group over-shadow the shared interests of other participating groups. The majority group then tells the others on what grounds they may participate or partake of items. That is not very democratic.

Democracy needs the free-willed participation of citizens to participate in their own rule. The sense of efficacy in a democratic environment is the greatest element in repelling intimidation. In a democratic environment, lots of people speaking up will do some good and that practice of free speech is essential as evidence of broad participation.

Structured legal procedures, reliable law enforcement, opportunity for public scrutiny, respect for reason, and a determination to be pro-active socially provide the opportunity to promote the sense of efficacy that each action will have an actual effect on society. The purpose of the U.S. Constitution is to establish the pattern for government. The threat of the possibility of the tyranny of the majority is countered by the Bill of Rights, instituted for the protection of all citizens, regardless of any minority status.

Structured democratic society recognizes the essential need of positive social conflict and then endorses the collaborative agreement on laws and procedures for conflict resolution. The advantage of collaboration is that the richness of diversity is cultivated to produce the fruits of a variety of considerations and new conceptual combinations.

Negotiation is at the heart of politics. Negotiation is the intent to make a trade that satisfies both parties in a dispute. If you think that you can elect a person to public office and that person must never yield on any issue, there will be no effective negotiation. Politicians cannot be absolutists because the game does not work that way.

When social structures break down, such as riots or rebellion, the consensus of collaboration has been destroyed.

Prepare to Win

When the leader is inconsistent with the values for the use of authority, trust is destroyed, along with consensus, leading to tyranny by the leader. Restoring order by rule of physical force may gain peacefulness, but will not achieve consensus.

Positional authority is effective power as long as the source of authority, and its subsystems, maintain efficacy as perceived by the constituents. Positional authority alone, with no input from, or benefit to the constituency, is insufficient to achieve a loyal and participative democracy.

The amount of consensus on regulations and procedures acts to diminish the likelihood of dangerous political opportunity. Favoritism cannot continue under transparent regulatory scrutiny. Hence, the value of public disclosure and of a free press.

Welcome positive conflict.

If you hate conflict, go live in a cabin in the mountains. People who live in a society always have conflict happening. It can be a good and essential thing. Without social conflict there would be no social change. Everyone would be content with things as they are and no progress would ever be attempted.

The crucial issue is that for good things to happen, conflict must be creative conflict, not toxic conflict. It is toxic conflict that people avoid, and rightly so. Toxic conflict criticizes, tears down, ridicules, demotivates, lies, and grabs power. This is seen as the dark side of politics.

The light side of politics and creative conflict requires a diverse group of participants, open discussion, open mindedness, valuations of options and a desire to make things better. The power to enact agreement on improvement is shared, as collaboration bears the fruit of consensus.

Ground rules, or norms, for effective collaboration can be constructed by the group, and can be posted on the wall for reference. They may include practical agreements on how participants will treat each other. Only one person speaks at a time. There will be no personal attacks. All comments will be phrased in a positive statement. Time constraints will be observed. A process monitor will interrupt if any norms are violated. Members are permitted to request attention if they feel their comment was not validated.

These positive elements can be taught, and should be reviewed often, to keep them in the forefront of awareness. They are the basis of good collaboration. Of course, when more people can speak up and more ideas are put on the table, it takes longer. The more people feel that they had a chance to be heard, and had a chance to hear more from others, the more the eventual decision is then, hopefully, an amalgamation. Our representative form of government is ultimately designed to find broad based agreement.

By all means, make sure that you have positive conflict in your management team. People who never oppose an idea originating from the boss are mere decorations. People who say, "Now wait a minute, what about this contingency?" are like an insurance policy against dumb decision making. Your team should help you to face your challenges before money and momentum are at stake.

So if you are avoiding an issue in order to avoid conflict, become proactive in staging the issue in positive conflict. Establish ground rules for a positive environment. Solicit the involvement of people more likely to criticize anything they were not a party to, but don't let them outnumber the people who are more likely to bring good ideas. Appoint a neutral person to remind them of the positive comment rule when they speak negatively.

It is reassuring to offer to take notes on poster size paper and put them on the wall. Then participants can review items that have already been processed, and avoid repetition. Afterwards, participants may appreciate a written collection of all the posted comments. It is a form of group memory.

You may have internal conflict about a particular issue. Self-doubt or self-protection of your ego are luxuries that active people cannot afford. You need to do the best possible thing in each situation, making a careful decision and then move on with it. Of course, it is realistic to expect other people to have ideas that are sometimes as good as yours. If their idea makes sense, make history. Action makes history. Make action.

Leaders among the legitimate **elite** work to champion the principles of an effective democracy. They understand **profoundly** the many forces of power which work to maintain or change society. And the best of those leaders seek **brilliance** to gain innovation and consensus for the common good.

Prepare to Win

"Conflict, Power and Politics" from a biblical point of view.

Jesus did not live in a homogeneous village. In his world, there were the poor and the sick. There was unsafe travel. There were occupying military and government forces. There was a Jewish king living under that foreign dominance. There were classes of Jewish religious groups. There were religious hypocrites. There were other religions. There were other nationalities in opposition to the Jews. There were people with several wives and slavery was common.

Was this a terrible situation to bring the Lord into? No, it was a great time. The domination of the Roman Army provided a level of civil peace within the culture. The recent dominance of the Greeks provided a rich language that was almost universal in usage. What more do you need in order to "go and teach"?

Is the twenty-first century a good time to "go and teach"? With the near universal usage of the English language and the broad accessibility of the internet and social media, isn't this also a good time to "go and teach"?

Is there too much attention on political conflict in our culture? Are political issues distracting our attention? Is there too much worldliness and corruption? Do we rehash issues too much on talk radio or television? Does all of that take time and attention away from the command "Go and teach"?

In our culture, today, do we spend time worrying about the political viability of our witness in laws and in courts, to the detriment that we do not actually go out through the front door to "go and teach" in an active ministry?

Prepare to Win

Is our political activism in opposition to abortion so strong that we overlook taking time to understand and care for the teenaged girls? Would more girls be better off if we were better at obeying the command "Go and teach"?

Having godly citizens run for office in spite of the mud they must endure during a campaign is laudable. However, we need a hundred times as many non-candidates to be hands-on in intervention ministries for people at risk of living a life without God's generous blessing. Millions of campaign advertising dollars could have been used to intervene for the people the politicians say they want to help. Of course we should "Go and vote" but it is even more important to "Go and teach".

Whether we minister effectively to others is all about relationships. How about your relationships? Do interpersonal conflicts stop you from advancing the Gospel? How do you deal with conflict when it's personal with you?

Your first priority relationship should be to God. Sin short-circuits God's power to work through you. Confess your sins. Perhaps a triple-decker confession would be a good pattern for you. Here's how it goes.

First, admit that what you did really was a sin. Own up to it. Look clearly at it and call it what it is, bad, sin.

Second, acknowledge your regret and acknowledge that you grieved your Heavenly Father. If you have no remorse and if you cannot understand that God was grieved about your behavior, you have not really repented. You have to repent.

Prepare to Win

Third, resolve, to the best of your redeemed humanness, to once again be dependent on the Holy Spirit to will and to work through you for His good pleasure (II Corinthians 9:8).

How do you resolve conflicts with others? Use the same triple-decker confession. Work on defining the issues and their underlying motivations. Do you need to make a triple-decker confession to the other person? After that, go back to the decision making section of this book and work on solution criteria and an implementation plan to restore your relationship. Restore peace. It is good for brothers to be at peace with each other (II Corinthians 13:11). Then God can use you again to "go and teach".

The test is this: If you think differences have been taken care of, can you pray for your former adversary and can they pray for you, as the two of you bow your heads for prayer together?

What if trying to work things out does not work? If nothing gets resolved, you are to bless those who persecute you (Romans 12:14). As a child of the King, undeservedly blessed with every spiritual blessing, you can afford to be generous. Paul said he returned a curse with a blessing (I Corinthians 4:12). Someone who would deliberately hurt you really needs supernatural help. They need a heart transplant. They need pity. They need prayer. They need conversion. They need someone like you to help them to grow in Christian maturity.

Prepare to Win

Your thoughts:

Chapter 10: Realignments, Alliances and Growth

A strategy is a plan of action, which sometimes includes additional contingency plans. Strategists have an idea of advance chess moves. They know when to call on the artillery in battle. They know how to play one group against another group in political scenarios.

Strategic planning is the practice of getting group consensus on planning given events and using the group to provide the wisdom of a multitude of counselors. The group also provides anonymity for individuals when blame may result. Got a tough decision? Send it to a committee.

When you send it to committee, you are just accessing the will of the people, but you have little control, so it is best if your attitude is just hoping that the committee comes up with a solution, any solution, just to get the thing done. Remember that when you work to avoid blame when it turns out bad, you also are denied credit when it turns out good.

Prepare to Win

Courageous leaders are risk takers and they strategize to expedite things that committees might labor over at length. Courageous leaders are also more likely to keep actions more tightly aligned with clear vision for the organization. However, many people only respect risk-taking when things turn out well! This is not logical but it is realistic. So calculate your risks carefully.

Strategic use of technological advances have always provided people with power, and with power comes dominance and wealth. A city located on a route of major trade, like Venice, or like the fortified towers demanding a toll on the Rhine River, represent dominance. The ability of a nation with extensive water access, like Denmark, to be able to raise an army faster than land-locked neighbors was a technical advantage. Nobel with his dynamite mastered a technology that created great wealth.

In this century the ability to move information has taken away newspaper prominence and given people access by the internet to new broader and deeper levels of less reliable information. Technology power, in each of its replacement forms, moves only forward.

What strategies are you currently working on?

What contingency plans do you have already? For example, all schools must annually update a school safety plan in case any of a number of perils happen.

Prepare to Win

What is your strategy if the budget does not work out? What can you consolidate?

Strategic planning also includes budgeting. A budget is a plan for money. You can change it as time goes by. Just like other elements in the plan, you must frequently check on your numbers.

Prepare to Win

Realignments

Because change is continuous and technology only moves forward, strategic planning sometimes hits a crisis. The scenario of unexpected events calls for drastic action. Major shifts are needed to avoid catastrophic events. Those shifts may demand abrupt realignments.

Realignments are like moving from one train track to an adjacent track. Recently, a failure to realign was notable with the Kodak Corporation. After a century of prominence in the imaging industry, they filed for Chapter 11 bankruptcy, and sold off several corporate divisions. Imaging had changed to computer technology, leaving any commitments to chemical processing insignificant.

Even the field of optics changed. Now cameras can have telephoto lens effects performed either optically or digitally. Beyond that, cell phones are replacing the cameras. Subscription emails are replacing printed newsletters. Blu-ray/DVDs have replaced VCR tapes, which replaced video discs which replaced 8 millimeter films.

If you have been making your living with a one-hour photo processing machine, what will you do with a future in a digital photography world? Will you stay with the machine and find other custom print needs, or will you stay with the industry and accommodate digital technology? That is a strategy decision about realignment.

Can you see what the next challenge to your enterprise might be?

Prepare to Win

Do you have a strategic contingency plan?

What types of realignments are you presently coping with?

What realignments do you perceive may be needed soon?

With what strategy will that shift take place?

How will you move the organizational culture to embrace the leap?

Are you in the process of retraining yourself and your associates to adapt to an apparent need to update your skills and technology?

Is the purpose statement for your organization broad enough that you can maintain your essential identity even with drastic changes in the expression of your services?

Alliances

Along with realignments, alliances may be a strategy that is new to your group. Alliances provide auxiliary support. With an alliance, the stability of a partner organization or subsidiary provides the depth and expertise that would take too long to develop within your own organization, but is at the same time complementary to your requirements.

The goal with alliances is to develop interdependence, to be able to count on support and provide that support to the alliance partner. If either partner has a monopoly the relationship is just that of a dependent customer, easily abused. If a partner cannot be relied on the relationship is just that of a commodity broker, easily abandoned.

Outsourcing happens, and it happens for several reasons. When you need a task done, any tasker can do it. It does not matter if the tasker is a temp inside your company or if the worker works for another allied company. However, when you need a team to work together, to develop shared understanding, to accomplish agreements, to keep short lines of supervision, to retain the company vision, outsourcing is positively the wrong choice.

How can you strengthen partners for a more permanent and interdependent alliance?

How can you keep suppliers from smothering you as the only source of key goods?

How can you do it quickly, carefully and cleverly?

Growth

By brilliant insight, based on profound grounding, you have identified your activity as among the elite in the industry. What will you do to build and grow?

Consider the lessons of franchisers. Franchisees need to stay true to the product or service. Research and development has been done in a controlled environment and released only after passing careful scrutiny. The franchise service or product is designed for faithful replication, not innovation.

At the same time, the franchise employees out in the field gain insight from observing the results of the tried and true. Their input, while perhaps less scientific, is validated by experience with the vast customer pool. It is true that their evidence is anecdotal, but it is actual evidence. Anecdotal evidence is often disdained because it is just not statistically useful. Anecdotal evidence actually does suggest valid research questions which can then be treated to a more statistically rich methodology. And even then, quantitative data need qualitative explanation.

The extent to which your endeavor grows is determined by many dimensions.

Is there broad demand (need) for the current product or service?

Is there validation of any intended improvements either by your research or by sample projects?

Prepare to Win

Or is there a series of modifications to tailor what you have so that it is operable in many discrete contexts?

Or can what you have or do be provided in expanding complexity to the same customers, like the ever-improving cell phones?

Will your suppliers and your alliances be able to keep pace with your expansion?

How will you act when your prosperity draws imitators and/or conceptual competitors eager to get one up on you?

Do you have business practices and people within your own organization with business maturity to deal with dynamic growth?

How will you acquire necessary capital to fund growth? How much will it require? How much will you sell to venture capital?

Where will you get the additional direction for your venture, such as a board of directors?

Start thinking about these issues now. You have to be ready.

Prepare to Win

Remember, to be among the **elite** is to be out in front with well managed growth. To be among the **profound** is to know the industry so well that you sense the winds of change and anticipate what your organization needs to address before others do. To be among the **brilliant** is to have your breakthrough strategy designed in a way that others have not yet developed.

Prepare to Win

"Realignments, alliances and growth" with a biblical view.

The greatest realignment in life is moving from darkness into the light, by changing your ultimate allegiance from self-centered devotion, and moving to a state of alignment with God and with the redeeming work of Jesus Christ.

Realigning with Jesus sets up an entirely new program of values and goals. It would be scary if a person were not assured that God loves them and that God would not be gentle with the transition. Many times the first thing a new believer needs is reassurance of God's love, as the new believer comes into a new awareness of the ugliness of sin.

A local group of believers, a church, is a good example of an alliance. The Bible says the purpose of a church is to build up the saints for the service of making the world a better place and inviting more people to make Jesus and his realignments the priority in their lives.

The church can be considered a supernatural alliance. It is filled with believers who have been given one or more spiritual gifts, so that together, interdependently, they have the strengths needed to be a functional group in order to accomplish spiritual goals (I Corinthians 12).

Finally, do you know how to multiply? When you share your faith with others, you multiply the number of people who glorify God. As they share the faith, the multiplication gets compounded. That is how Christianity spread so quickly in the first century. That is

Prepare to Win

how it should spread now. You can have a multiplier effect with sharing your faith, although you may not be able to see how far it extends. You may even be able to tactfully include your multiplication in work situations. It can be an adventure. Do not just keep the faith, share it.

Prepare to Win

Your thoughts:

Epilog: Ensuring a Lasting Legacy

What do you want your family and friends to say at your funeral? They probably won't be discussing your chemical compounds, or the first buy-out that got you started as a big wig.

Go back to your thoughts about your purpose in life. Then think about the opportunities you had to contribute beyond your work life. Did you make some?

How about hobbies? Have you taken time to really enjoy a hobby and let the distraction refresh your spirit?

Can you get away somewhere that business is the last thing you think about? Do you plan for that periodically?

Are you established enough to take a chunk of time each week and lend your mega-skills to strengthen a charity or a church?

Prepare to Win

Your life was not meant to be a slave to your work. Of course being consistent and responsible are good things. But most people have a lot of room to become more colorful, before anyone would call them "wild and crazy".

If your professional life is to be described as among the elite, profound and brilliant, why can't your personal life also be among the elite and the profound and the brilliant? You can be the leader among those you know and love, who strives to find new and better ways to build insight, hope, love and fun into their lives.

What better legacy to leave than that of a person who ardently and thoughtfully strove to make the most of every opportunity, both professionally and personally?

You really don't know how much time you have left. Why wait for death bed farewells? Not everyone gets a hospice period. Write a note to each person that you care about, expressing your love and your hopes for their life. You might consider making it an annual event, on every birthday you celebrate. Create a keepsake.

Prepare to Win

Your thoughts:

Prepare to Win

Your thoughts:

Prepare to Win

The Four Spiritual Laws

By Bill Bright

Just as there are physical laws that govern the physical universe, so are there spiritual laws that govern your relationship with God.

LAW 1: God **loves** you and offers a wonderful **plan** for your life.

God's Love
"God so loved the world that He gave His one and only Son, that whoever believes in Him shall not perish but have eternal life" (John 3:16, NIV).

God's Plan
[Christ speaking] "I came that they might have life, and might have it abundantly" [that it might be full and meaningful] (John 10:10).

Why is it that most people are not experiencing the abundant life? Because...

LAW 2: Man is **sinful** and **separated** from God.

Therefore, he cannot know and experience God's love and plan for his life.

Man Is Sinful

"All have sinned and fall short of the glory of God" (Romans 3:23).

Man was created to have fellowship with God; but, because of his own stubborn self-will, he chose to go his own independent way and fellowship with God was broken. This self-will, characterized by an attitude of active rebellion or passive indifference, is an evidence of what the Bible calls sin.

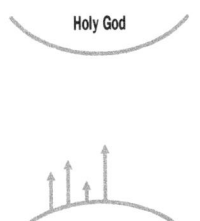

Man Is Separated

"The wages of sin is death" [spiritual separation from God] (Romans 6:23).

This diagram illustrates that God is holy and man is sinful. A great gulf separates the two. The arrows illustrate that man is continually trying to reach God and the abundant life through his own efforts, such as a good life, philosophy, or religion—but he inevitably fails.

The third law explains the only way to bridge this gulf...

Prepare to Win

LAW 3: Jesus Christ is God's **only** provision for man's sin. Through Him you can know and experience God's love and plan for your life.

He Died In Our Place
"God demonstrates His own love toward us, in that while we were yet sinners, Christ died for us" (Romans 5:8).

He Is the Only Way to God
"Jesus said to him, 'I am the way, and the truth, and the life; no one comes to the Father but through Me'" (John 14:6).

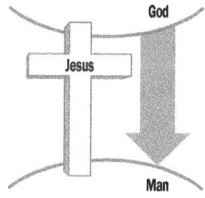

This diagram illustrates that God has bridged the gulf that separates us from Him by sending His Son, Jesus Christ, to die on the cross in our place to pay the penalty for our sins.

It is not enough just to know these three laws...

Prepare to Win

LAW 4: We must individually **receive** Jesus Christ as Savior and Lord; then we can know and experience God's love and plan for our lives.

We Must Receive Christ
"As many as received Him, to them He gave the right to become children of God, even to those who believe in His name" (John 1:12).

We Receive Christ Through Faith
"By grace you have been saved through faith; and that not of yourselves, it is the gift of God; not as a result of works that no one should boast" (Ephesians 2:8,9).

When We Receive Christ, We Experience a New Birth
(Read John 3:1-8.)

We Receive Christ Through Personal Invitation
[Christ speaking] "Behold, I stand at the door and knock; if any one hears My voice and opens the door, I will come in to him" (Revelation 3:20).

Receiving Christ involves turning to God from self (repentance) and trusting Christ to come into our lives to forgive our sins and to make us what He wants us to be. Just to agree intellectually that Jesus Christ is the Son of God and that He died on the cross for our sins is not enough. Nor is it enough to have an emotional experience. We receive Jesus Christ by faith, as an act of the will.

These two circles represent two kinds of lives:

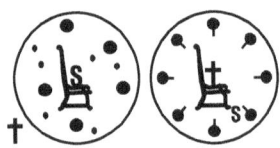

Which circle best represents your life?
Which circle would you like to have represent your life?

Prepare to Win

The following explains how you can receive Christ:

You Can Receive Christ Right Now by Faith Through Prayer
(Prayer is talking with God)

God knows your heart and is not so concerned with your words as He is with the attitude of your heart. The following is a suggested prayer:

> Lord Jesus, I need You. Thank You for dying on the cross for my sins. I open the door of my life and receive You as my Savior and Lord. Thank You for forgiving my sins and giving me eternal life. Take control of the throne of my life. Make me the kind of person You want me to be.

Does this prayer express the desire of your heart?

If it does, I invite you to pray this prayer right now, and Christ will come into your life, as He promised.

How to Know That Christ Is in Your Life

Did you receive Christ into your life? According to His promise in Revelation 3:20, where is Christ right now in relation to you? Christ said that He would come into your life. Would He mislead you? On what authority do you know that God has answered your prayer? (The trustworthiness of God Himself and His Word.)

The Bible Promises Eternal Life to All Who Receive Christ

"God has given us eternal life, and this life is in His Son. He who has the Son has the life; he who does not have the Son of God does not have the life" (1 John 5:11-13).

Thank God often that Christ is in your life and that He will never leave you (Hebrews 13:5). You can know on the basis of His promise that Christ lives in you and that you have eternal life from the very moment you invite Him in. He will not deceive you.

An important reminder...

Prepare to Win

Do Not Depend on Feelings
The promise of God's Word, the Bible—not our feelings—is our authority. The Christian lives by faith (trust) in the trustworthiness of God Himself and His Word. This train diagram illustrates the relationship among fact (God and His Word), faith (our trust in God and His Word), and feeling (the result of our faith and obedience). (Read John 14:21.)

The train will run with or without the caboose. However, it would be useless to attempt to pull the train by the caboose. In the same way, as Christians we do not depend on feelings or emotions, but we place our faith (trust) in the trustworthiness of God and the promises of His Word.

Now That You Have Received Christ
The moment you received Christ by faith, as an act of the will, many things happened, including the following:

Christ came into your life (Revelation 3:20; Colossians 1:27).
Your sins were forgiven (Colossians 1:14).
- You became a child of God (John 1:12).
- You received eternal life (John 5:24).
- You began the great adventure for which God created you
- (John 10:10).

Can you think of anything more wonderful that could happen to you than receiving Christ? Would you like to thank God in prayer right now for what He has done for you? By thanking God, you demonstrate your faith.

To enjoy your new life to the fullest...

Suggestions for Christian Growth
Spiritual growth results from trusting Jesus Christ. A life of faith will enable you to trust God increasingly with every detail of your life, and to practice the following:

- **G** Go to God in prayer daily (John 15:7).
- **R** Read God's Word daily (Acts 17:11); begin with the Gospel of John.
- **O** Obey God moment by moment (John 14:21).
- **W** Witness for Christ by your life and words (Matthew 4:19; John 15:8).
- **T** Trust God for every detail of your life (1 Peter 5:7).
- **H** Holy Spirit—allow Him to control and empower your daily life and witness (Galatians 5:16, 17; Acts 1:8; Ephesians 5:18).

Fellowship in a Good Church
God's Word instructs us not to forsake "the assembling of ourselves together" (Hebrews 10:25). If you do not belong to a church, do not wait to be invited. Take the initiative; call the pastor of a nearby church where Christ is honored and His Word is preached. Start this week, and make plans to attend regularly.

Used by permission. Copyright 2007 Bright Media Foundation and Campus Crusade for Christ (CCCI ®). Formerly Copyright 1965-2006 Campus Crusade for Christ, Inc. "Bright Media Foundation" is a registered trademark of Bright Media Foundation, Inc. "Campus Crusade for Christ International" and "CCCI" are registered trademarks of Campus Crusade for Christ, Inc. All rights reserved. No part of this book may be reproduced, stored in a retrieval system, or transmitted in any form or by any means, except in the case of brief quotations printed in articles or reviews, without prior permission in writing from the publisher.

Prepare to Win

Your response:

Author's Note:

If you would like to share some of your thoughts or questions with me, you may make contact this way: drdave@prepare-to-win.com. I am particularly eager to hear from you if you decided to establish a relationship with God after reading this material.

Your individual development may benefit by working in a paid coaching relationship. A coach is like a personal fitness trainer, except the coaching is about all you do, except exercise routines. Being accountable to someone else is extra insurance that you will actually and consistently make the efforts to change and improve. One of my Prepare-to-Win associates or I may be available to assist you with your personal and professional development.

Perhaps we may meet at a Prepare-to-Win workshop in a city near you. The prepare-to-win.com website will have updated information on those dates.

Thank you for reading this book. Although we have not yet met, you have my best wishes.

Dave Severson, Ed.D.

Prepare to Win

www.ingramcontent.com/pod-product-compliance
Lightning Source LLC
Chambersburg PA
CBHW061512180526
45171CB00001B/140